DRAWING LEGENDARY MONSTERS
DRAWING THE MINOTAUR
AND OTHER DEMIHUMANS

Steve Beaumont

FRANKLIN WATTS
LONDON•SYDNEY

Published in 2011 by Franklin Watts

Copyright © 2011 Arcturus Publishing Limited

Franklin Watts
338 Euston Road
London NW1 3BH

Franklin Watts Australia
Level 17/207 Kent Street
Sydney, NSW 2000

Artwork and text: Steve Beaumont and Dynamo Limited
Editors: Kate Overy and Joe Harris
Designer: Steve Flight

A CIP catalogue record for this book is available from the British Library

Dewey Decimal Classification Number: 743.8'7

ISBN: 978 1 4451 0454 6
SL001629EN

Printed in China

Franklin Watts is a division of Hachette Children's Books,
an Hachette Livre UK company.
www.hachettelivre.co.uk

CONTENTS

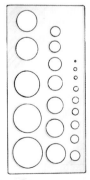

GETTING STARTED

Before you can start creating fantastic artwork, you need some basic equipment. Take a look at this guide to help you get started.

PAPER

Layout Paper

It's a good idea to buy inexpensive plain A4 or A3 paper from a stationery shop for all of your practice work. Most professional illustrators use cheaper paper for basic layouts and practice sketches, before producing their final artworks on more costly material.

Cartridge Paper

This is heavy-duty, high-quality drawing paper, ideal for your final drawings. You don't have to buy the most expensive brand – most art or craft shops will stock their own brand or a student range. Unless you're thinking of turning professional, this will do just fine.

Watercolour Paper

This paper is made from 100 per cent cotton, so it is much higher quality than wood-based paper. Most art shops stock a large range of weights and sizes. Either 250 grams per square metre (gsm) or 300 gsm will be fine.

PENCILS

Buy a variety of graphite (lead) pencils ranging from soft (6B) to hard (2H). Hard pencils last longer and leave less lead on the paper. Soft pencils leave more lead and wear down quickly. HB pencils are a good medium option to start with. Spend time drawing with each pencil and get used to its qualities.

Another product to try is the mechanical pencil, where you click the lead down the barrel using the button at the top. Try 0.5 mm lead thickness to start with. These pencils are good for fine detail work.

CIRCLE TEMPLATE

This is useful for drawing small circles.

FRENCH CURVES

These are available in several shapes and sizes, and are useful for drawing curves.

INKING AND COLOURING

Once you have finished your pencil drawing, you need to add ink and colour. Here are some tools you can use to achieve different results.

PENS
There are plenty of high-quality pens on the market these days that will do a decent job of inking. It's important to experiment with a range of different ones to decide which you find the most comfortable to work with.

You may find you end up using a combination of pens to produce your finished artworks. Remember to use a pen with watertight ink if you want to colour your illustrations with a watercolour or ink wash. It's usually a good idea to use watertight ink anyway as there's nothing worse than having your nicely inked drawing ruined by an accidental drop of water!

PANTONE MARKERS
These are versatile, double-ended pens that give solid, bright colours. You can use them as normal marker pens or with a brush and a little water like a watercolour pen.

BRUSHES
Some artists like to use a fine brush for inking linework. This takes a bit more practice and patience to master, but the results can be very satisfying. If you want to try your hand at brushwork, you should invest in some high-quality sable brushes.

WATERCOLOURS AND GOUACHE
Most art stores stock a wide range of these products from professional to student quality.

MASTERCLASS: DEMIHUMANS

THE HORSE-LIKE CENTAUR

All of the creatures in this section are a hybrid (mix) of human and animal features. Although the head of the centaur has a human appearance, it still has characteristics that separate it from being purely human. This exercise will show you how to change the shape and appearance of the human face to create a demihuman.

Picture 1 Start with an oval. Then draw lines to roughly work out where the eyes, nose and mouth will sit.

Picture 2 Next add the face. The eyes are set at a slight angle to indicate a point of difference from a human.

Picture 3 Draw the pointed ears. Instead of human ears, the centaur has ears more like those of a horse.

Picture 4 Next work on the hair. Note how it flows like a wild horse's mane. Remove the construction lines.

Picture 5 Finally shade in the hair leaving sections of white for highlights. Also add shading to the face, particularly around the eyes.

The centaur is now a hybrid of a horse and a human but with his own unique identity.

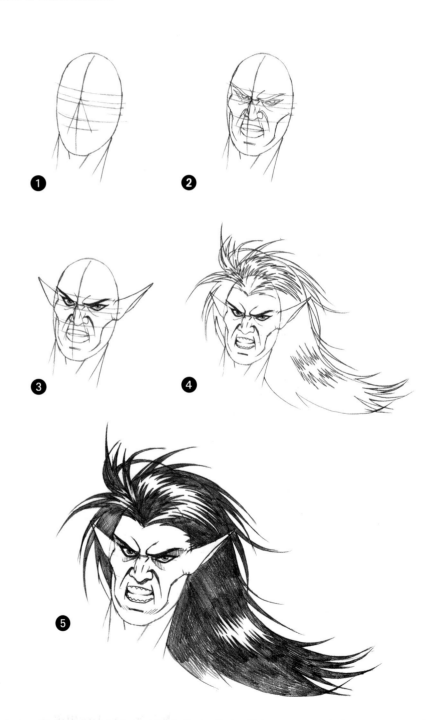

THE FELINE SPHINX

The Sphinx is a feminine hybrid of a lioness and a human, with the wings of an eagle. Check out the tips below to help you draw her cat-like face and decorative headdress.

Picture 1 Start with an oval shape for the head, then map out the eyes, nose and mouth.

Picture 2 Next add detail to the face. The eyes are turned inwards and set at an angle. A real cat has round eyes but this is a fantasy character so we can use the approach shown here to create a cat-like effect.

Picture 3 The four ornaments around the top of the headdress are snakes. Notice how they are all S-shaped. The snake at the front is a cobra.

THE BULL-LIKE MINOTAUR

The Minotaur is half-human and half-bull. Below we show you how to draw his stocky frame.

Picture 1 shows the hind legs of a bull. In Picture 2 you can see that the construction of the bull's leg is similar to that of the hind leg of a horse. This basic leg shape will form the lower half of the Minotaur. In Picture 3 we have simplified the legs so they have a semi-human appearance. We have drawn the knees heavily bent and made them muscular.

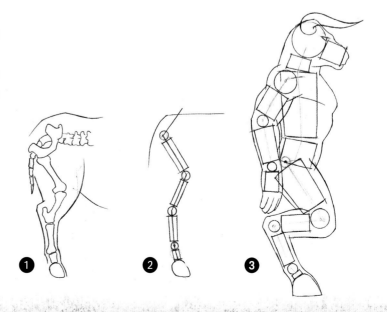

CENTAUR

Half-human creatures are found throughout myth and legend. According to Greek mythology, centaurs are fast-moving, free-spirited creatures that are part-human and part-horse. They could be wise teachers, or savage warriors. They were believed to have taught hunting techniques to humans.

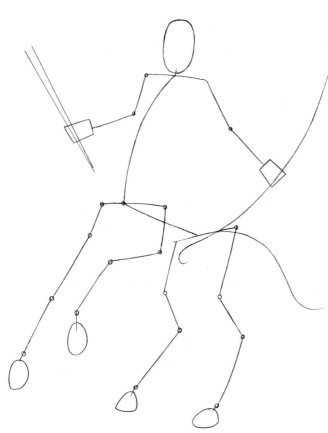

❶
Begin with the stick figure. Remember the top half is human and the bottom half is a horse. Make sure you include the hooves.

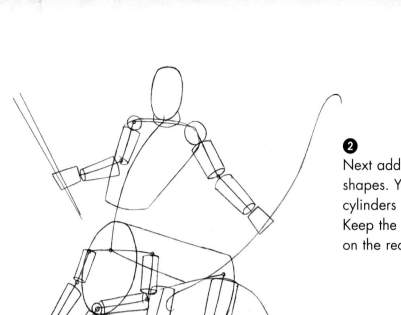

2
Next add the construction shapes. You are mainly using cylinders in this drawing. Keep the cylinders wide on the rear legs at the top.

3
Sketch the angry face and pointed ears. Then add the skin by drawing around the construction shapes. The tail should flick outwards.

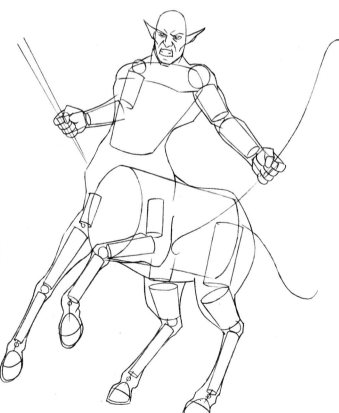

4

Erase the construction shapes, then draw the centaur's bow and arrows. Notice how the bow has a snake's head at the top. Keep the lines of the arrows straight. Add the flowing hair, body armour and horse's tail.

5

Shade your drawing. Pay particular attention to the underside of the centaur's hair, chest and tail. Leave areas of the hair white to create highlights. Add fine detail to the face.

You'll discover lots of tips on page 6 to help you draw a striking face for the centaur.

6

Ink over the pencil lines. Tackle the small details on the centaur's body carefully so the patterns remain well defined.

7
Go over your drawing in colour. We've used a cool palette to create a moody feel.

A mixture of blue and grey for the hair adds an otherworldly quality.

Start with a pale skin tone for the upper body. On top, use a warmer skin tone to bring out the muscles.

For the lower body, try a base layer of cool grey followed by darker grey. Include hints of pale blue.

13

SPHINX

In Greek mythology, the Sphinx attempted to pass on her wisdom to mortals through riddles, but devoured those who were unable to give the correct answers. Eventually she was defeated by the Theban hero, Oedipus. He solved her riddle and was made king for destroying the monster.

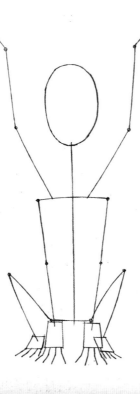

1

Start with the stick figure. Notice the Sphinx is in a sitting position. Make sure the wings stretch high above the head.

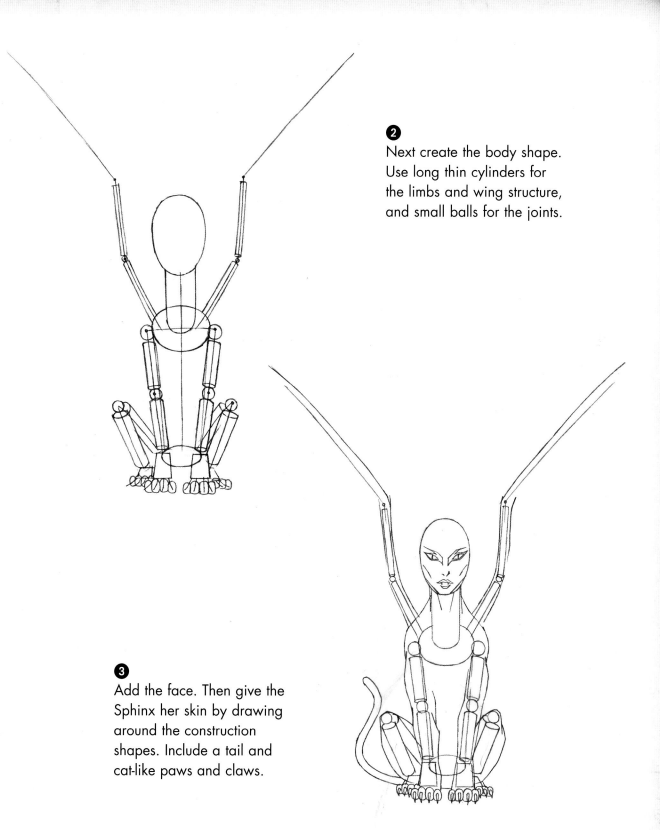

② Next create the body shape. Use long thin cylinders for the limbs and wing structure, and small balls for the joints.

③ Add the face. Then give the Sphinx her skin by drawing around the construction shapes. Include a tail and cat-like paws and claws.

Check out page 7 for instructions on how to create the face of the Sphinx.

4

Rub out the construction shapes. Then add the ornate headdress, necklace and snake bangles. Build the wings by layering the feathers.

5
Now shade the lower belly and hind legs to create a sense of depth between the front and back paws. Include shading on the feathers and claws to give them definition. Add fine detail to the jewellery.

TOP TIP
Varying the strength of your ink lines will add interest and depth to your final drawing.

6
Apply ink over the pencil drawing. Keep the lines of the necklace as straight as you can. Notice how the brows cast a shadow over the inner eye.

SPHINX

7 Bring your art to life by adding colour. Start with a beige base over the whole area.

Use a pale skin tone for the ghostly face and rich yellow for the spooky cat's eyes. A turquoise mouth will make the Sphinx look even icier.

Build up interest by applying layers of colour. Use shades of sand, yellow and brown.

Colour the gold jewellery with sandy and yellowy brown. For the gemstones, use a jade-green colour to create contrast.

MINOTAUR

The most savage demihuman was the Minotaur. This half-man, half-bull monster was so fearsome that the king of Crete locked him inside a labyrinth. Each year seven young men and seven young women were sent into the labyrinth as a sacrifice to this man-eating creature. Eventually it was slain by Theseus, with the sword of Aegeus.

❶ Start with the stick figure. You need curved lines for the horns and ovals for the clumpy feet. Don't draw the fingers on the Minotaur's left hand. It's easier to add these later, gripping the axe.

2

Build the body using chunky cuboids and wide cylinders. Form the axe with a large oval and a straight, angled line for the handle.

TOP TIP
Although the Minotaur has a bull's head, you can give his face more character by mixing in human features. This is a useful technique for many fantasy creatures.

3

Draw the face and goat-like beard. Then add the skin outline. Shape the feet into cloven hooves using upside-down V-shapes. Improve the axe.

Go to page 7 for more tips on how to draw a Minotaur's stocky bull-like body.

TOP TIP
Many illustrators use references from books or the internet to help make their drawings accurate.
This Minotaur is holding a Viking axe but you could choose a different object.

4
Erase the construction shapes. Then add the fur and muscles, paying attention to the contours of the arms, chest and legs. Add detail to the axe and draw the fingers around the handle. Give the Minotaur his studded wristcuffs and earrings.

5 Finish the pencil drawing with fine detail to the body. Shade the areas you will be inking heavily in the next step.

6

Now ink your artwork.
Use solid areas of ink to add
drama and to emphasise the
Minotaur's bulk.

MINOTAUR

7

Start your colour work with a base layer of beige. Include hints of green and grey.

The axe is coloured blue-grey. A darker grey is used for the shading.

Brick beige was used to colour the horns.

Build up the skin with cool tones. We've used layers of green-brown and grey.

Warm tones work well for the rich furry mane. Try brown mixed with red.

CREATING A SCENE: THE LABYRINTH

According to Greek mythology, the Minotaur's labyrinth was so vast and complex that it was virtually impossible for anyone to find their way out once they were inside. As they wandered through its corridors in a state of increasing confusion, the huge half-human monster who lived there would patiently track them down. Now here's your opportunity to recreate that scary scene...

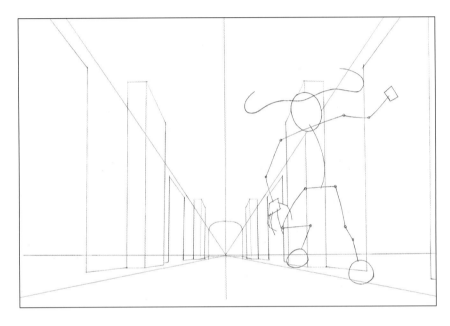

1 In a large indoor space like this, perspective becomes crucially important. Draw lines of perspective coming together at a vanishing point to give the impression of the labyrinth being a vast location that disappears well beyond our current view.

2 Now you can start to 'build' the walls of your labyrinth. Remember that the bricks in the walls must also follow the lines of perspective. Add in simple curves for the various overhead arches.

3 Add more detail to your brickwork. Try to keep the edges of bricks a little ragged to help create the weathered look of an underground labyrinth. The paved floor works in the same way as the walls – just follow those perspective lines.

4 Now add some shading. The labyrinth is supposed to be a dark and frightening place, so bear this in mind, adding more layers of shading the further back you get to help create that sinister atmosphere.

5 The inking stage will use a layering of darker areas to help add depth to the image as the tunnels disappear into the depths. Start off lighter at the front and build the layers as you move back. Remember it is always easier to add lines than it is to take them away.

28

6 Building colour depth is important here. Start with a lighter colour and then use a complementary, darker colour to build the recesses of the labyrinth. A minimal use of colour will help to keep the focus on the main character while drawing the eye towards the more forbidding rear of the image at the same time.

GLOSSARY

cuboid
An object that has six faces like a cube.

cylinder
A shape with circular ends and straight sides.

demihuman
A mythological creature which is half-person and half-animal.

highlight
A light, bright area in a picture.

hybrid
A cross between two different things.

ornate
Detailed and complicated.

perspective
Changing the size and shape of objects in an artwork to create a sense of nearness or distance.

turquoise
A colour midway between blue and green.

vanishing point
The point at which the lines showing perspective in a drawing meet each other.

INDEX

WEBSITES

http://www.elfwood.com/farp/art.html
A collection of articles about drawing characters and scenes from myth and fantasy.

http://drawsketch.about.com/od/drawfantasyandscifi/tp/imagination.htm
Advice on drawing from your imagination.